GOOD TABLE MANNERS

The Child's World

Published by The Child's World®
1980 Lookout Drive • Mankato, MN 56003-1705
800-599-READ • www.childsworld.com

Acknowledgments
The Child's World®: Mary Berendes, Publishing Director
The Design Lab: Design and production
Red Line Editorial: Editorial direction

ISBN 9781614732303
LCCN 2012932469

Printed in the United States of America
Mankato, MN
July 2012
PA02126

ABOUT THE AUTHOR

Ann Ingalls writes stories and poems for people of all ages as well as resource materials for parents and teachers. She was a teacher for many years and enjoys working with children. When she isn't writing, she enjoys spending time with her family and friends, traveling, reading, knitting, and playing with her cats.

ABOUT THE ILLUSTRATOR

Ronnie Rooney took art classes constantly as a child. She was always drawing and painting at her mom's kitchen table. She got her BFA in painting from the University of Massachusetts at Amherst and her MFA in Illustration from Savannah College of Art and Design in Savannah, Georgia. She now lives and works in Fort Lewis, Washington. Her plan is to pass her love of art and sports on to her two young children.

CONTENTS

Welcoming Guests...4

Sitting at the Table...6

Wait Your Turn...8

All That Silverware...10

A Mouthful...12

Finger Food?...14

No Thanks!...16

After You Eat...18

A Bit More Polite...20

Quick Quiz...22

Glossary...24

Books and Web Sites...24

Index...24

Welcoming Guests

When guests come to your house, greet them at the door. Place their coats on hangers. Do not toss them in a big wad on the floor. Shake their hands and hug **relatives**. Even hug Aunt Edna who has stinky breath and false teeth.

Sitting at the Table

Be a pal. Pull a chair out for a lady. Hold it steady while she scoots up to the table.

Find your seat and sit up straight near the table. Place your napkin on your lap. Do not plop your elbows on the table. You do not want to look like a **barbarian** at a feast.

Did You KNOW?

In France, it is rude to have your hands under the table. Hands should be above the table at all times.

Wait Your Turn

Wait for everyone to be served. Hosts should pick up their forks before you begin eating. Do not reach for food across the table. Pass food to your left. And take only as much as you think you can eat. Do not pile a mountain of mashed potatoes on your plate!

Did You KNOW?

It's polite for guests to eat first in Afghanistan. They should also eat the most.

All That Silverware

Sometimes you will see extra knives and forks. Some are even above the plates. Use the outside fork first. And do not use your knife to pick the food out of your teeth.

Bread plates are placed to the left of your dinner plate. Choose a piece of bread or a roll. Tear or cut off a bit. Then put butter on that piece. Don't try to tear it apart with your teeth. Crumbs might fly across the table!

A Mouthful

It is not polite to talk or chomp with your mouth full. Do not stuff too much in. You can do all of these things when you are at a hot dog eating contest—just not at Grandma's table.

Bring food from the plate to your mouth. Do not drop your face into your bowl. Leave that move for Rover!

And if you have to leave the table to go to the bathroom, place your napkin on your chair. Say, "Please excuse me."

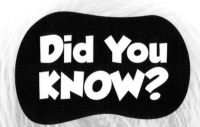

Did You KNOW?

If you are dining in China, don't eat all the food on your plate. Your host will think you are rude! Leaving a little makes you a good guest.

13

Finger Food?

Do not slurp or lick your fingers. Who wants to listen to that? It is a no-no to stick your finger in cake icing, no matter how good it looks. And do not dip your chip twice in the ranch dip. No one wants your germs!

Only eat with your fingers if the food is supposed to be eaten that way. Don't grab your pork chop like a cave man. But pick up your tacos. It also depends on where you are. Even French fries are eaten with a fork at fancy restaurants.

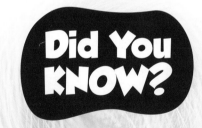

Did You KNOW?

In Japan, slurping your noodle soup is a good thing! It is even better to slurp really loudly. It tells your host that you are thankful for the good meal.

No Thanks!

Learn how to refuse a food politely. Not everyone likes the same things. If it is a new food, try a tiny bite. You might like it more than you think. If you do not feel like eating fish eggs or frog legs, it is better to say, "No, thank you." Do not say, "That food smells rotten!" You might hurt the host's feelings.

Remember that it takes a lot of effort to make dinner for guests. Think of that before you say something bad about the food.

After You Eat

The meal is done. Now what? Say something nice to the cook and the host. Thank them for the delicious food. If the food tasted yucky to you, you could say, "The flowers on the table are so pretty."

Wait to be **excused** from the table. Until then, stay seated. Listen to what guests are talking about. Join in if you like.

It is fun being a guest, right? Don't forget! You should always thank your host for asking you to dinner.

A Bit More Polite

Now you know which fork to use. You know which way to pass the pasta. Before long, you will wow everyone with your great table manners. You might even be **invited** back for dinner.

Practice your manners to make them **perfect**. Before long, your manners will be finger-licking good!

Quick QUIZ

Put your new table manners in action with this pop quiz! Will you choose the right rules?

The best time to begin eating is when:

a. the food comes to the table.
b. the clock in the front hall begins to chime.
c. you feel like it.
d. everyone has been served and your hosts pick up their forks.

When you want someone to pass the green beans, you should:

a. shove others out of the way and go get them yourself.
b. run around the table and scream, "Give me the green beans!"
c. say, "Please pass me the green beans."
d. throw yourself down on the ground and have a screaming fit.

The best way to pass food around the table is to:

a. throw rolls one by one to each person.
b. put the food in the middle of the table and let people grab it.
c. put the food back in the kitchen. Say, "If you want it, go get it."
d. pass it to your left.

To tidy up at the dinner table, be sure to:

a. wipe your mouth and fingers on your shirt.
b. wipe your mouth and fingers on the tablecloth.
c. use a napkin to wipe your mouth and fingers.
d. pick the food out of your teeth with a knife.

If you did not like the food your host served, you can say:

a. "Next time, let's order pizza."
b. "This was yucky. I'll bring a sandwich next time."
c. "Thanks for inviting me."
d. "Couldn't you think of something better to serve?"

If you want to act like a barbarian, you can:

a. talk with your mouth full.
b. stuff too much food in your mouth.
c. chomp with your mouth open.
d. do all of the above.

Please do not write in the book!

Glossary

barbarian (bar-BAIR-ee-uhn): A barbarian is a person who is wild and without manners. A barbarian has horrible table manners.

excused (ek-SKYOOZD): When you are excused, you are given permission to not do something. Were you excused from the table?

invited (in-VITE-id): To be invited is to be asked to do something or go somewhere. Marcy invited me over for dinner!

perfect (PUR-fikt): Something that is perfect does not have any flaws or mistakes. My table manners are perfect now.

polite (puh-LITE): To be polite is to have good manners. It is polite to put your napkin on your lap.

relatives (REL-uh-tivz): Relatives are members of your family. It is fun to have dinner with relatives.

Web Sites

Visit our Web site for links about table manners: **childsworld.com/links**

Note to Parents, Teachers, and Librarians: We routinely verify our Web links to make sure they are safe and active sites. So encourage your readers to check them out!

Books

Burstein, John. *Manners, Please!: Why It Pays to be Polite.* New York: Crabtree, 2011.

Eberly, Sheryl. *365 Manners Kids Should Know: Games, Activities, and Other Fun Ways to Help Children Learn Etiquette.* New York: Three Rivers Press, 2001.

Espeland, Pamela. *Dude, That's Rude!* Minneapolis, MN: Free Spirit Publishing, 2007.

Index

Afghanistan, 8
China, 12
eating, 8, 12, 16
fingers, 15
France, 7
Japan, 15

napkin, 7, 12
refusing food, 16
silverware, 11
sitting, 7
thanking hosts, 15, 19
welcoming guests, 4